MW01248527

CHRISTMAS
GREETINGS

CHRISTMAS
GREETINGS

CHRISTMAS
GREETINGS

CHRISTMAS
GREETINGS

CHRISTMAS
GREETINGS

CHRISTMAS
GREETINGS

CHRISTMAS GREETINGS

CHRISTMAS
GREETINGS

CHRISTMAS
GREETINGS

CHRISTMAS
GREETINGS

CHRISTMAS
GREETINGS

CHRISTMAS
GREETINGS

CHRISTMAS
GREETINGS

CHRISTMAS
GREETINGS

CHRISTMAS
GREETINGS

CHRISTMAS
GREETINGS

CHRISTMAS
GREETINGS

CHRISTMAS GREETINGS

CHRISTMAS GREETINGS

CHRISTMAS
GREETINGS

CHRISTMAS GREETINGS

CHRISTMAS
GREETINGS

CHRISTMAS
GREETINGS

CHRISTMAS GREETINGS

CHRISTMAS
GREETINGS

CHRISTMAS
GREETINGS

CHRISTMAS
GREETINGS

CHRISTMAS
GREETINGS

CHRISTMAS
GREETINGS

CHRISTMAS GREETINGS

CHRISTMAS
GREETINGS

CHRISTMAS
GREETINGS

CHRISTMAS
GREETINGS

CHRISTMAS
GREETINGS

CHRISTMAS
GREETINGS

CHRISTMAS
GREETINGS

CHRISTMAS
GREETINGS

CHRISTMAS
GREETINGS

CHRISTMAS
GREETINGS

CHRISTMAS
GREETINGS

CHRISTMAS
GREETINGS

CHRISTMAS
GREETINGS

CHRISTMAS
GREETINGS

CHRISTMAS
GREETINGS

CHRISTMAS GREETINGS

CHRISTMAS
GREETINGS

CHRISTMAS
GREETINGS

CHRISTMAS
GREETINGS

CHRISTMAS
GREETINGS

CHRISTMAS
GREETINGS

CHRISTMAS
GREETINGS

CHRISTMAS GREETINGS

CHRISTMAS
GREETINGS

CHRISTMAS GREETINGS

CHRISTMAS
GREETINGS

CHRISTMAS GREETINGS

Printed in the USA
CPSIA information can be obtained
at www.ICGtesting.com
LVHW051936170524
780600LV00002B/391